Cecil Helman

THE EXPLODING
NEWSPAPER

and Other Fables

The Menard Press

THE EXPLODING NEWSPAPER
and Other Fables
© 1980 Cecil Helman
All Rights Reserved
ISBN: 0 903400 51 0
Cover design by Neil J Crawford
The Menard Press is a member of ALP
Menard Press books are distributed in North America by SPD:
Small Press Distribution, 1636 Ocean View Avenue, Kensington,
California 94707, USA

The Menard Press
23 Fitzwarren Gardens
London N19 3TR
England

To L. and R. and S. and I.

Set in 11pt Baskerville by Cecil Woolf Typesetting, 1 Mornington
Place, London NW1 7RP and printed for the publishers by
Rotaflow Ltd, 5-25 Scrutton Street, London EC2A 4HJ

Contents

3

Acknowledgements

Acknowledgements are due to the editors of the books and journals where many of these fables first appeared:

U.S.A.: Tree, Kayak, California Quarterly, San Francisco Phoenix, Famous, Boxcar, Heirs International, Montana Gothic, and Strange Faeces.
Britain: Ambit, Iron, Other Times, Fix, Monsieur Dada, and Mirror Image.
South Africa: Contrast, and The Purple Renoster.
Canada: Titmouse
France: Paris Voices
Denmark: Pearl

Others have been published in the following anthologies:

U.S.A.: *The Prose Poem: An International Anthology—* ed. by Michael Benedikt; Dell, New York, 1976.
Imperial Messages: One Hundred Modern Parables — ed. by Howard Schwartz; Avon Books, New York, 1976.
Panjandrum Number 5— ed. by Denis Koran, Panjandrum Books, San Francisco, 1977.
South Africa: *Quarry 76: New South African Writing* and *Quarry 77* — ed. by Lionel Abrahams & Walter Saunders; A. Donker, Johannesburg, 1976 & 1977.

Eight of the Fables have previously appeared in another collection:

The Emperor's Aversion, and Other Fables — Cecil Helman; Caligula Books, London, 1977.

1
The Exploding Newspaper

One morning, a marmalade-eating man opens his break-
fast newspaper and reads in it the following headlines—
EXPLODING NEWSPAPER—FULL STORY!—WIDOW-
ED WIFE TELLS ALL!—and underneath—

'Exclusive—At eight o'clock yesterday morning, or
even earlier, an ordinary-looking newspaper of the
type that he usually reads, was delivered to Mr Fred-
erick Ferble of 51 Fernley Road. Except for his wife
Mrs Mabel Ferble, Mr Ferble was alone in the house
at the time. Sitting at the breakfast table, chewing on
marmaladed toast, Mr Ferble commenced to read this
newspaper. What happened next was dramatically des-
cribed by Mrs Ferble—"he was reading aloud from
the paper," she says, "about a man someplace who
reads a report in a paper about an exploding news-
paper, and then, a few minutes later—the paper *he's*
reading begins to tick, then blows up Bang in his hand!
just like that—Well, he was still rambling on about all
this and what it might mean," recalls Mrs Ferble,
"while I went into the kitchen to check on this tick-
tocking sound I could hear (thought it must be the
kettle, boiling over) when suddenly a tremendous
VaBoom! and the paper explodes and so does poor
Frederick. All I can remember was a Whooooosh! and
a bang of smoke and then there was nothing left of
him but his green woolly socks (which I'd knitted
only the week before). Poor Frederick Ferble, it was
a terrible tragedy". "I myself wasn't hurt," she added,
but the carpet's absolutely ruined."

'City authorities are still investigating the incident,
but so far nothing satisfactory by way of explanation
has been found.'

The man crackles the newspaper, then turns to the
War Crises on the next page. 'More marmalade, dear?'
asks his curly wife, a pink floral blob on the other side
of the table. She slides the sticky bottle towards him.

5

'Uuumph' he says, speaking like a fried egg, his eyes wandering over the headlines. Somewhere in the background the kettle bubbles. 'Can't you take that clock away?' says the man, 'it's getting on my nerves'—'Clock? We haven't got a clock—'A second's silence. Tick-Tick-Tick— They jump shrieking for the door—But, too late! VABOOM!! an explosion rips through the marmalade bottles, scattering big black headlines over the walls; WAR! CRISIS! HORROR! and EXPLOSION! crack the ceilings and shatter the window panes. The room fills with tinkling glass, with the smoke and debris of Sensational News Items . . . .

But that was only the beginning. Since that day they have become even more frequent, these exploding newspapers. No house, no suburb is safe from them any more. In every home the news is exploding at the breakfast tables; a panic is creeping through the cities. We open the papers with terror in the mornings, afraid of what might happen—perhaps an explosion, perhaps even worse—perhaps to read of a typhoon, and a moment later it rises from the pages, ripping the roof of your house away; or news of China, and the room is crowded suddenly with short yellow soldiers sniping at the budgerigars. News of war brings shock troops battling on the breakfast table, their bullets plopping into the porridge. Currency Crises by the thousand clutter the kitchens of suburbia, among omelettes and marmalade. On almost every front lawn, these days, heavy astronauts can be seen—moonwalking—

Of course none of us dares buy a newspaper any more, for fear of what we might read. Every day we ask one another—Is it safe yet to read the news? But no one knows the answer; nor is there any way of knowing it. Only by buying the paper, and reading the latest news, can we ever hope to find out . . . .

2
The Unmasking of the Apocalypse

for Nanos

On the day before the Apocalypse, the streets are strewn with discarded masks.

We step among the piles of torn paper masks, their cheeks gaily painted, scattering in the winds. With them lie the plastic and professional masks of judges, officials and others; some stern, some with frozen frowns, others still plumply benevolent. In the dusk running feet crunch the porcelain masks of fashionable women, and trip on the hessian faces of the poor. One by one we peel off the masks from our faces, tear off the smiles and sneers, moulded in rubber or wood, and throw them out of the windows. In the streets they are collected and carried to bonfires, where soon the flames flicker up through their mouths and empty eyeholes. Everywhere in the smoke there are the clicks of locks unlocking as people unhinge their black iron masks and throw them heavily to the ground. Silence deadens the thud of their falling . . . .

As the twilight of the last day reddens, we see—and recognise—one another for the first time, for the last time. Now only one mask—different from all the others—remains glued to our faces. It is that strong transparent mask which we can see only on others, not on ourselves; which we can pull from the faces of our friends, but not from our own. Within this final mask the air thickens slowly in our lungs. Our eyes meet in the dusk; we reach out across the voids between us. But our fingers are clumsy in the dark, and the mask is tightly glued. As we struggle and fumble we know that if only we can remove it now, the Apocalypse may never—need never—arrive.

3

The Library Madonna *for Ruth*

Screaming with terror behind the smile of a dead madonna, she looks up over my shoulder at her old friend, the ceiling, and says:—'When you touch me, I feel a pink blush flowing through my body—I've become pink clay, and you're moulding me back into Myself again'—I touch her high cheekbones and sad black hair, and we listen again to her Genealogy: she is, she says, the only and unknown descendant of a Finnish princess and a poor Jewish violinist—born of their couplings in locked and long-ago ghetto rooms somewhere inside her mind—'I have known better times—' says her finger now, pressed tightly against my lips—

Now she stands behind the counters in suburban libraries, moving between my bed and the library shelves with the smudged grace of a ruined countess working in a poor bordello—

She lives in a room in an old house on the mountain-side, alone with all her paperbacks—with torn blankets—yellowed music scores—and shrieks and falling furniture filling the other rooms. From there she sends me:—sudden tins of Twining Tea—unknown Mongolian love-poems of the 3rd Dynasty—a white rose, bottled in honey—the breast feathers of her dead canary—herbs, picked at midnight—and half-empty postcards, written in mysterious code.

Lying each night on the mountain-side, dissolved in her body and black eyes, she sculpts and carves me—with quick frowns, and unusual smiles—into characters plucked from her paperback novels—and lays me between the pages, flat and dry as a pressed flower—then strokes her creation, sighs, and looks away—Long sighs, dark eyes—and sad bridges between us. O my pale friend, floating on painted toenails high above the ground—

Weeks later, at the very end, your midnight silences over the phone—'Love—it must be winter already—in the water I've seen my goldfish cry—'

4

The Marriage in the Marsh

Please don't think I'm in any way prejudiced against him. On the contrary, like any father I'm concerned only for my daughter's happiness. She is, after all, our only child, and since we moved here to the house in the marsh before she was born, she had a lonely and friendless childhood. Also, we live a very isolated life here; there is a vast distance between us and the next family, and sometimes months or even years will pass before we see another human being. And even then they rarely stay longer than a day or two, before the snakes, the bubbling of the marshes, and the warm dampness of the long evenings drive them away. Yet her mother and I had always hoped that one day when she was old enough to choose, she would find herself a husband who would make her really happy. It's true she has had quite a few boy-friends already, but somehow each of them has been, in one way or another—well, a little bit strange. That's why, when she mentioned to us one suppertime that finally she'd fallen in love, and what's more that she was going to get married, we were naturally very anxious to meet our prospective son-in-law, especially as for the first time in many years she really seemed to be happy. We wondered at the time why we had never met him before, if they'd been going about together, but as we try not to pry too much into her life, we just assumed that per-haps she had met him on one of her morning walks through the marshes around the house.

A few nights later he came to dinner for the first time. My wife had cooked some of her finest dishes, taking special care to avoid using any meat as we'd heard that he preferred vegetarian food. Long before he arrived the table had been laid with our best silver cutlery, and the house was filled with the savoury smells of soups and frying mushrooms.

Well, I must say that when we first saw him we were rather surprised, my wife especially, though he was extremely polite to both of us, and he and our daughter really seemed fond of each other. From the way she looked at him I knew that whatever we thought about it, she was determined that they would get married. The meal that night, though quite well cooked, (especially the lentil soup), was still rather tense for all of us. He didn't say much, nor did my wife, and in a way I was quite relieved when he had gone, and my daughter gone up to bed. As soon as we were sure that she was asleep, we rushed over to the bookcases—as we usually do in situations like these—and spent the night searching through the books and encyclopaedias that we'd brought with us to the marsh. Early in the morning we came across a photograph in one of the books that confirmed our worst suspicions. There was no doubt about it—it had an amazing resemblance to our daughter's fiancé; if it wasn't a picture of him then it was certainly of someone in his family. The caption underneath confirmed what I'd thought all along—well, to get to the point, his family *definitely* have a foreign-sounding name. And though I'm not saying that he himself wasn't born in these parts, there's no doubt at all that originally he comes of foreigner stock. And that's what has got us worried. As I said, we're not prejudiced against foreigners, or against him, but we do feel that 'Like needs Like', as they say. It's always easier if you come from similar backgrounds, as we've often said to her about some of her other boy-friends.

And then there's something else about him which worries us—he is, how shall I put it, extremely big; one might even call him enormous. On the evening he came for dinner he occupied almost all of the dining room, and the lounge as well, and my wife had to squeeze around him to get into the kitchen. Then there's his colour—he's green; not bright green, you understand, just a sort of dull olive colour with ugly little green spots all over his body. Well, as they say, 'Love is blind', but still, when I see him next to my pretty little daughter (and he's almost twelve times her height) it really hurts me inside. Also, I know he tries to be careful when he comes here, but almost every time he's left something broken in the house. My wife won't forgive him easily for breaking her china teapot last week with his tail, or for leaving his great muddy footprints on the carpets. As for myself, I try to be tolerant of his ways, if only for my daughter's sake, but somehow we don't seem to get on very well together. I specially climbed up his neck last week to have a proper man-to-man talk with him, but fell off when I was only half way up. Almost broke my neck in the process, but he didn't say a thing; didn't seem to mind a damn what happened to me. And that's not all—there's another thing about him which we find irritating, not to say offensive—he doesn't wash—never! He's always covered with this thick black marsh-mud all the way up to his belly, which he rubs off onto our furniture, and that doesn't smell too pleasant I can tell you.

Well, three days ago, things finally came to a head. There was an awful scene in the kitchen with much screaming and throwing of plates. We tried to explain to our daughter that obviously they weren't compatible, he being a foreigner and all that, and that she shouldn't see him ever again. After that we didn't have a moment's peace; she lay weeping in her room, refusing to eat or drink, refusing even to speak to us. As for her boyfriend, we couldn't get him to forget about it either. At nights we could hear him thrashing about outside, ripping up the huge trees around the house and flinging them into the marsh, trampling the garden into a soggy mess, and smashing down the fences. The whole house shook with his roars and trampling, shattering most of the downstairs windows. I kept the front door locked securely, of course, but he broke it with his tail as though it were made of paper. Finally, in a violent fit of rage one night he ate three of the dogs, both cows, and at least fourteen of our best imported chickens. From under the bed where we were hiding, we could hear the shrieking and the slow crunching of bones right underneath our window.

After that, of course, we gave in—after all, what else could we have done? They are going to be married in one week's time, and our daughter will become Mrs Brontosaurus. Looking at them now, I must admit that they do look a happy couple together; she seems to love him, and hangs from his neck in a most affectionate way. And in time, I suppose, we'll get to like him too, though it'll be more difficult for my wife to adjust to him than for me to. In these matters I'm much more easy-going, you see.

We haven't met his family yet; he says they live 'somewhere in the marsh', but is vague as to exactly where. He says they are all travelling to our house—forty or more of them—to be here in time for the wedding.

We expect them to arrive any day from now.

5
The Grocery Shop

A customer in a suburban grocery shop asks, please could he buy a tinned man. It is an unusual request and the grocer tells him so. He sells men in cardboard boxes, in cardboard cartons, and even in disposable plastic containers, but tinned man he does not stock. In fact the idea offends him; he is anxious not to lose a good customer so doesn't say anything. But secretly he wonders how the customer could expect a man to survive without air in a metal tin, no matter how much food he has with him. He suggests instead a new product which he has recently begun selling, and which has been widely advertised on television. It consists of a married couple complete with furniture and a caged canary, attractively packaged in a large cardboard box. The manufacturers include a written guarantee that the people enclosed are in reality legally married. And they even promise a full refund if this is proved to be untrue. A special offer, shortly to expire, offers a free month's supply of birdseed as well as food for the couple, with every box bought. The customer listens to what the grocer is saying but keeps silent. He peers through the barred windows of the box at the two elderly people inside. The old woman is feeding the canary, while the man sits slumped on the floor. They glance up towards him, then look quickly away. The customer searches frowning through the money in his pockets and wallet. No, he says at last, no I'm afraid I don't have enough with me; they're too expensive. And besides, they're in a box; it's the tinned variety I'm looking for, not the ones in cardboard or plastic. Perhaps I'll try the supermarket. He leaves thanking, before the grocer can stop him. He has lost a customer and is furious. He picks up the big metal plate on which has been heaped the couple's food for the day, and throws it violently into the street. They rush to the window of their box, pressing their red faces against the bars and pleading shrilly with him for their food. But he ignores their shouts and walks back to the front of the shop where a customer is asking for a tin of ravioli . . . . . .

6
The Plastic Pyramid

The President had a plastic pyramid built specially for himself. It towers high over the city. Flat triangular surfaces, transparent as water, reflect the sunlight. Deep within its clear volume is the inner burial chamber, constructed as a cube of orange perspex. Inside this lies a raised glass coffin on a bier of varnished amber. The initials of the late President, in gold and interlocked italics, decorate the slopes of the pyramid, the four walls and roof of the burial chamber. Here he was put to rest, carefully embalmed, and the pyramid resealed amid our sorrow. Through the layers of plastic, perspex and glass we could see the President's body, dressed in the uniform of Commander-in-Chief—the grey uniform he most wore when addressing the people. He was in every way as we remembered him. Medals and decorations refracted the daylight off his chest. In his left hand he held the eagle standard and flag of our Republic. In front of the bier a battery of many microphones waited in silence. He had ordered, very emphatically, that we should assemble to see him every day, to listen as he spoke to us silently through the dead microphones. But his successors in the Presidency have long ignored his last orders. The daily crowds have withered away in time, now few remain. Those faithful still living are too blind to see even beyond their own eyelids. Over the years thieves have burnt through the plastic with acetylene lamps, cut their way into the perspex burial chamber. They have stolen the President's medals, and even taken away his bones. Microphones dangle broken from the bier. The scratched surfaces of the empty pyramid are pierced with zig-zag holes, radiating cracks at their edges. Fragments of plastic and glass litter the floors, among open tins and crumpled newspapers. One of these newspapers, recent and grease-stained, tells of an enormous glass pyramid which the new President has ordered to be built. It will be higher and clearer than any other one in the world. The microphones for this pyramid, says the paper, have already been ordered.

Then a wind, whistling through plastic, blows the paper out into the deserted streets. . . .

7
The Millionaire's Fire

A fire breaks out in the millionaire's mansion. All of its thousand rooms are in danger. At first only the living quarters are ablaze, but soon the flames crackle along the tapestries into the remaining nine hundred where the millionaire's money is stored. For Christ's sake call the city fire brigade! shrieks his tinted wife. From the city? No! Nonsense! says the millionaire, think of all the money they've cost me—meaning by the 'they' in that remark his own private fire-brigade, stationed permanently in the grounds of his estate. Shortly thereafter these fire engines arrive, with a whiny sirening, hurtling down the driveway towards the house. Each man, hand-picked, wears a tailored velvet uniform, gold buttons and braid, with the millionaire's initials tattoed on his left forearm. They jump from the engines, shouting their war cries, and point their hoses up at the flaming windows. Each hose is enclosed in its own embroidered cover; while the red engines—, in baroque style—have murals of sheep and shepherdesses painted on their sides, enscrolled in gold and lapis lazuli. Pre-recorded Mozart is piped out of a portable gramophone. Under the millionaire's direction the engines pump jets of champagne (Möet et Chandon of '81) onto the blazing house, while a few send arcs of pasteurized milk playing over the roof-tops. But the flames burst from room to room; the gilt ceilings fall in a chorus of crackles and hisses. Nothing burns easier than stacked-up money; and soon nine hundred rooms swelling with banknotes are metamorphosed, almost miraculously, into nine hundred cubic piles of smoking ashes. Among them champagne bubbles fizz in time to a Mozart sonata. With a cry the millionaire rips off his wife's emerald earrings, swallows them down, and runs shrieking into the bushes.

Only a few days later, a garden of new and exotic plants, well watered by milk and champagne, blooms and flowers among the blackened ruins . . . . . .

8
The Revolution of the Pinball Machines

The pinball machines make a revolution. They burst out of the corners of cafes, and break down the locked doors of amusement palaces. They tear the cords which plug them to walls all around the city. Soon they have formed a procession and clank down the High Street together. At their head is 'Las Vegas', whose painted lights flash as the silver ball tring-trings onto ten-thousand-points and a Free-Replay. Behind him jostle a machine named 'Gunsmoke' with five-hundred-and-nineteen points, and another 'Olympics' with only a hundred and a broken flipper. The others are shabbier, their glass cracked and taped together, bearing the stigmata of cigarette burns on their legs and sides. Their flippers flash, bells tring rhythmically, while red and yellow lights pulsate across their backs. Around them follow groups of young men, trying awkwardly for a final game, but the machines refuse them; their slots accept no more coins, nor ever will again. The cafes they have left are crowded with consternation. People gather round the empty spaces in their corners, handling the broken cords hanging from the walls. Soon they are deserted, as are the palaces of amusement. Angry and frustrated men roam the streets. They break into the City Hall, which is being besieged by the pinball machines, and seize the mayor whom they blame for the revolution. They force him to eat sixpences and paint 'Las Vegas' on his forehead in yellow and red. 'Gunsmoke' and 'Olympics' applaud what the men have done by ringing up fifty-points more apiece, but the rest of the machines are not placated. With lights pulsating and trailing their broken wires behind them, they move angrily off. The revolution goes on.

9
The Cellist

I've forgotten her name, but she played me between plump thighs like an antique cello.

She was a cellist from an academy, with sad Jewish eyes and shiny boots. And eyeshadow of blue neon, and long sighs lined with potato latkes. Soulful as a second-hand piano, she was.

I was lonely at the time, a solo performer.

One night she knocked on my door, dressed only in a glance, and our concert was arranged on the spot. We did a duet, of her own composition, plucked from my skin with fat fingernails. A complex fugue it was, with twists and tremolos, and at its crescendo cheers burst from every corner of the mattress.

She was content, and sighed over me like a million grandmothers.

Night went, and the next morning I gently peeled her off me, like elastoplast from a healed sore.

Later, when I was alone again, I found she'd left me our music-score—written in red blood semiquavers all over the sheet—

10
The Leper's Tale

I am not a Leper, said the man with the dry and cratered face, but a fragment broken off the Moon who has floated down to Earth. See the mountains across my back, and the valleys, he said. There are many of us fragments, scattered like limbless meteorites under your feet. Some, like myself, have fallen into the grounds of hospitals. But even so—as each month ends most of us will die, and must float away again to reassemble the New Moon, piece by piece.

It is sad to be only a piece of a puzzle, added the Leper, as he drifted up over my head, and into the dusk . . . .

11
The Dark Childhood of the Bats

Huge bats sweep down from the night and carry us away in their tight hairy fists. We fly over deserted cities, held by our hair under their black rubbery wings. After a while, we resign ourselves to what has happened and start imitating the squeaks of our carriers, flapping our arms, and searching the clouds for insects to eat.

None of us can remember any existence before this night; or before our childhood, begun in the moist darkness of caves, hanging from the ceilings . . . .

12
The Farmer's Daughter

I was new to the countryside, a travelling salesman selling needles to hide in haystacks. She was a farmer's daughter. And her father was away, she said, cycling on a bicycle towards the planet Jupiter, where her mother lived.

I was surprised at this, but she bought one needle from me and, blushing redder than a sunburnt radish, sewed both my shoes to the floor; so I stayed with her.

We were alone on a sudden square field, embroidered with woollen weeds. Our cabin floated in a pineforest, suspended between two tall days; outside it was winter. She had warm freckles, I remember, and it must have been her birthday that night, for she blew me long rubber balloons in which I lay, watching as red candlelights set on the horizon.

In the darkness she mistook me, I think, for a newly-picked banana; for a hairy sheep; a cow to be milked; a bronco, bucking; a gallop of horses; one million snorting bulls; and a shrill migration of geese. While I, lost on a pink and unfamiliar landscape, mistook her for:—a soft meadow, newly ploughed; an irregular hill; a clump of oyster trees; some quicksands; thunder rumbling; a lightning flash; and the rapid palpitations of an earth tremor.

The room was chaotic with squeals and squawks, and echoing snorts, and the frantic gabbles of geese—

Then suddenly, we struck it rich—I felt the hot WHOOSH! of an oil well, gushing richly from the middle of the meadow; and droplets of oil falling, like silences, all over the forest.

That was my first lesson in agriculture, that was.

13
The Oldest Photograph in the World

The oldest photograph in the world has just been discovered in a tomb in Alexandria. It's thousands of years old, say the experts, perhaps even more.

It shows an elderly man with a white beard and cloak, surrounded by hundreds of grey-robed midgets.

Some archaeologists, who've examined the blurred photograph, think that this may be a photo of the original 'Old Man' or 'Old Master' of all mythologies; who crops up in the history of every culture as their first Great Teacher, each time telling a similar message, but under a different name—calling himself 'Socrates' or 'Confucius', 'Lao-Tsu' or 'Moses', 'Abraham', 'Muhammad', or 'Ghotama the Buddha'. And who apparently travelled through all the countries of the world, spreading his wisdom, sometime in the early days of History. They think that the photo was taken on a visit made by this Master-of-Many-Names to his disciples in Mesopotamia and Egypt; also that the midgets are not midgets at all, but normal-sized people, and therefore that the Master . . . .

But, whatever the truth of their explanations, there *is* something familiar about the Master's blurred face and enigmatic smile. Where have we seen it before? Maybe as a face in an afternoon crowd, or in a newspaper headline, or in our dreams perhaps—?

There is something else unexplained about the photograph—the large round Mirror held in the Master's right hand, in which can be seen reflected the upturned faces of each one of the midgets . . . .

14
The Endless Opposition of Teng and Tong

In the very beginning, says an old Chinese legend, when God gave birth to the Earth, he offered it as a gift to his Right Hand called Teng. It was a curious object, this gift, spherical in shape with a granulated surface. Under the microscopic eye of Teng it was curiouser still, for the surface consisted of browns and blues, and on the browns small bipedal creatures could be seen gathered here and there in opposing groups. From time to time one of these groups would rush on the other and beat them to the ground, or else be themselves beaten to the ground. This seemed to be occurring all over the surface of the sphere. For this reason, and the apparent uselessness of the gift, the Right Hand Teng flung it disgustedly away in the general direction of God's Left Hand—Tong. As is well known, the Left and Right Hands of God are in constant opposition and competition, of which typhoons, tornadoes, and tidal waves are constant proof. Therefore, the thought of presenting Tong with a useless and absurd gift tickled the tips of Teng's fingers with tentative amusement. However, as the Legend continues, Tong was no more pleased than he was with this ridiculous ball, and flung it furiously back in the direction of Right Hand Teng. Who—immediately on catching it—punched it back again with a venomous swipe—

And this, the Legend concludes, has continued to this very day, ever since the Earth was born. The Earth's unfortunate sphere is thrown from the Right Hand of God to His Left, and back again and to and fro, thudding backwards and forwards for all eternity.

To this day the Chinese commemorate the rejection of the Earth and its endless oscillation between the two Hands of God, by a strange ritual which involves the violent punching of a white sphere, representing the Earth, between two persons standing opposite one another. Like other Oriental rituals it has been exported to the West, in a distorted form, and here it is known, in translation, as 'The-Great-Cosmic-Flight-Of-The-Earth-Between-The-Two-Hands-Of-God-Forwards-And-Backwards', or else in the original Chinese form as 'Ping-Pong'.

15
The Enigmatic Sounds of Broken Teeth

In a small fairground tent, under the blinking fluor-
escent sign—'PRINCE ZAMPARO: FORTUNE-TELLER'
—a Gypsy with broken teeth and large silver earrings,
examines the palm of a client, throws the Tarot, glances
in a glass ball, and with a sigh makes the following pre-
dictions:

> 'You will find yourself suddenly in a fairground. You
> will be drawn to a small tent under a neon sign. On
> the sign will be written in red letters the words
> 'PRINCE ZAMPARO: FORTUNE-TELLER'. Then
> you will enter the tent, and sit down at a table with a
> Gypsy. This Gypsy, who is Zamparo himself, has
> only the ruins of teeth in his mouth. Also he wears,
> hanging from both his ears, large silver earrings. He
> will carefully examine your palm, throw the Tarot
> cards, and look into a small glass ball on the table.
> From time to time, Zamparo will look up to you,
> then sigh. Finally, when he has finished, and you wait
> for his predictions, he will say—nothing. He will tell
> you words, but will remain silent—even if you threaten
> him. You will get up, pay, and walk out of the tent.'

The man rises from the table, pays the Gypsy with
the crackle of notes, and walks out of the tent. To his
amazement, he finds himself in the middle of a fairground,
among coloured stands and caravans. There are balloons
everywhere, and the shrieks of children. Quite suddenly,
he has an impulse to have his fortune told. He searches
through the fairground, perhaps for many hours but can-
not find any trace of a fortune-teller, nor of a Gypsy
tent or caravan. Eventually he gives up the search, and
with his head heavy with frowns counts the money in his
pocket, and walks slowly home . . . .

16

The True Legend of St.George and the Dragon

He was horribly deformed, was St George, from early years on, in a way which people found most repulsive. For one thing, he had a tail—which might have been acceptable, had it not been green and pointed at the end. Also he had scales all over his body, and when angry breathed fire through both his nostrils. From teeth to tail, he was forty-three-and-a-half feet long, when fully grown. But however grotesque, the Saint's subsequent Martyrdom made up for it all in the eyes of the early Church, as shown by his canonization. You will recall, from the Legend, his cataclysmic battle with the Demon-Dragon Beezedek, sent by Satan to Earth in the helmeted guise of the Knight, Sir Roderick Fey; how nobody saw through Beezedek's disguise, until it was much too late; how, in a flash, seven-hundred-and-fifteen of George's fellow villagers were electrocuted by evil currents from Sir Roderick's laser-lance; how the outcast George flung his huge clumsy body onto the tip of the lance, short-circuiting it, and blowing Beezedek's evil fuse-box for all time; and, how all that remained of poor George was a pile of moist green ashes, and an acrid smell . . .

To this day, George's impalement and electric Martyrdom are commemorated in plethoras of paintings entitled 'Saint George and the Dragon', hanging in art museums and in the carpeted halls of the Vatican.

17
The Riddle of the Black Forest

A man wakes up one morning to find himself lying in the shadows of a greasy dark Forest. The trees of this Forest are black and thin, without branches, and curiously coiled at the ends; and a warm and smelly mist—which makes him retch—hangs between them like an old cobweb. He is lying among tiny pink toadstools scattered between the trees, on pale ground covered with moisture. Quick earth-tremors ripple through the Forest, bending the trees from side to side . . .

The man wanders among the trees searching for friends, but cannot find anyone. Eventually he pulls himself up one of the trees, and hangs precariously from its coiled end. Now he can see that he's woken in the middle of an enormous black Forest, and through the steam clouds rising from among the trees he can make out a range of high pallid hills, surrounding the Forest on all sides.

There is something familiar about this Moist Forest, thinks the man, swinging thoughtfully from side to side.

He is tortured by metaphysical Questions:—Am I Alone In The Forest? Are There Other Such Forests In The Universe, And If So Are Any Of Them Inhabited? Whose Forest Is It, And Who Created It? These and other Questions buzz and whirr around his head chasing one another, but they can never catch an Answer.

Sometimes it's difficult to speculate on the universe, while hanging from a hair inside a Huge, Sweaty Armpit— Whosoever's it is . . . .

18
The Diagnoses Parachuted from the Sky

On a sudden bespectacled morning, one thousand Psychiatrists are parachuted with their beards into the city. They run shrieking through the streets, flinging the citizens down on to rapidly-inflatable rubber couches, and stamping diagnoses onto their foreheads. The quick twitchings of their ball-point pens echo among the skyscrapers.

Well, we've become used to this sort of thing over the years, believe me, and our ambulance men know exactly what to do:— armed with lassoos they comb the city, rounding up the Psychiatrists and gently carrying them away to the waiting convalescent homes . . .

Some time later—with the ink still wet on their foreheads—each Psychiatrist is handed a re-packed parachute and a free chocolate ice-cream, and then loaded aboard aircraft heading for faraway cities—As they take off, we can still catch their giggles and shrieks fading in the roar of the turbojets . . . .

19
The Poets and the Flower

The news spreads quickly, flashing across the screens—for the first time in years, say the bulletins, a flower has been found in the city! No one still living can remember when last this has happened. The citizens come crowding from all around to see the phenomenon. People shove and push against policemen pushing and shoving them back. What they can see is a tiny flower blooming from a crack in the concrete, in an alley leading from an abattoir. Its four grey and brittle petals dangle from a spindly stalk, their scent muffled by the smog. Ooooooh and Aaaaaaaah say the crowd, Aaaaaaah! and Oooooooh!

When the scientists have finished their examination, and the television cameras taken away, the Government circles the flower with barbed wire and erects a special museum around it. Now mobs of poets, hungry for the sight of a real flower, jostle and punch at the entrances. To control them, the Government issues special Poetry Permits which certify that Poet Number. . . . . , Name. . . . . is entitled (after deleting which is not applicable) to One Quarter/One Half/or One Full Hour of inspiration time at the aforementioned flower. Once inside the poets sit in bearded rows; fog of their heavy breathing drifts among the barbs of the barbed wire. Ballpoint pens run rhyming across the pads resting over their knees. Thin poets who have not yet experienced the flower, queue and cough impatiently outside. Cough cough let us in, they shout pallidly.

Soon shelves of libraries swell with poems, with poetry, with poetry anthologies in praise of the flower. Each of its petals has dedicated to it several symphonies, sonatas, an opera, and at least one play. But everyone—even the Government—knows that this cannot continue for long . . . .

One night, at last, four pale poets disguised as the Museum Director, break into the museum itself. They cut through the barbed wire barricade and carry the flower away. Later in a candlelit cellar, with flames flickering under their cheekbones, they cut off the petals, tearfully embrace one another—then swallow them down in a mystic communion. All the candles are extinguished by their scent.

While the secret police search through all the candle-lit cellars in the city, the Government secretly substitutes a model of wire and painted cardboard for the flower. It is a good copy, but the plan fails. They are forced to call in ambulances from neighbouring cities to carry away the poets who sprawl in fainting heaps around the cardboard flower. These recuperate in special wards in the city hospital, where they are consoled by re-reading again all the flowery poems they wrote in the past. Only the Chief State Poet himself, anxious to retain his licence, remains to write sonnets in praise of its painted petals.

Eventually in time the four pale poets are trapped, caught, tried, condemned, caged in a cage in the city square. Led by the secret police, the people pelt them with old lithographs; only the other poets keep away from the square. One early morning the dawnlight falls through the bars onto a tableau of glory. The four young poets stand frozen like a forest; from their beards and fingertips grow gardens of purple, red, and blue flowers, with luxuriant leaves rustling in the winds. Buds slowly open and blossom across the cage, their petals refracting the sunlight in rainbows of colour. Sweet scents drift again through the streets of the city . . . .

20
The Court of the Clockwork Judges

To speed up the process of Justice, the latest Clockwork Judges have just been installed in all the courtrooms in the city.

They arrive in crates marked 'Judges', unloaded among clapping crowds by Orderlies with twirly moustaches. Once inside the courtrooms and the palaces of justice, the crates are opened, blue tissue wrappings unwrapped, and the parts of the Judges fitted together; pieces of plastic and tin, coils of electrical wire, and dozens of tiny lightbulbs are all carefully assembled according to the Instruction Manual. When assembled they stand on four spindly legs screwed to the floor—each one a box, roughly rectangular in shape, above which a vertical panel pulsates with multi-coloured neon lights and numbers.

When they've been painted a sombre black, (in accordance with Paragraph 3, Article 5 of Act Number 31B)—and one installed in every courtroom—the Judges are plugged into the walls, switched on, and the first of the Cases begins:—

CASE NUMBER 1A—a man is accused of kicking his refrigerator. . . He lies now, thin and whimpering, chained to the middle of the courtroom floor.

The courtroom is crowded. Standing on either side of the Judge, the Prosecutor and Defending Counsel bow slightly to one another, then slip their coins into the slot in his side, and with loud shouts of 'LONG LIVE JUSTICE!!' together push in blue button 'A'—(as described in the Instruction Manual). The Judges' panel lights up yellow, framed in a vivid neon; at the buzz of a buzzer all the spectators stand, then sit again at the ring of a bell. Now the trial proper begins—

A silver ball bounces up into the glass-covered box; Defence and Prosecution lean panting heavily over the

Judge, jabbing at their buttons marked 'B'. At every jab plastic flippers flip the ball this way then that. It whizzes across the box from side to side, driven around and around; lightbulbs flash across the panel, and the bells tring-tring with every bounce of the ball. Spectators jostle around them, cheering on first one lawyer, then the other. Then, suddenly, the ball—knocked across by the Prosecutor's flipper—drops down into the hole below the Defence's button. A bell trings wildly. There is consternation in the court; the Defence has lost the first point of the Trial!

On the floor the Defendant writhes and moans, but everyone ignores him.

Nine balls later his fate is decided—the Prosecutor has seven points, the Defence Counsel three. The case is over.

Almost immediately the buzzer buzzes again and all in the court rise for sentence to be passed. There is a hush in the room as the machinery clicks and whirrs. 'TRING!-TRING!-TRING!-TRING!' rings the Judge electronically;—'4!4!4!4!' pulsates in neon on the vertical panel above, throwing a bluish glow onto the whimpering face of the guilty man.

Ooooh! Four years' jail!! squeal the spectators to one another, giggling quietly.

Now four heavy men in black cardboard hats, each with a paper daffodil in his left lapel, enter the courtroom and move towards the convicted man. Just before they take him away, a huge tapestry of hills and shepherdesses drops down automatically from a slot in the ceiling. The Prosecutor, Defence, and the Prisoner are each handed a pink plastic flower by a court official. Arm in arm in a smiling group, they are photographed against this pastoral backdrop for the Court Records by the Official Court Photographer. Click!-Flash!-Click! go the cameras. Then quickly the court is cleared of everyone, and the Prisoner is dragged away. An Orderly cranks the backdrop up into the ceiling, and unplugs the Judge from the wall. He walks out of the room, locking the door behind him.

The first of the Clockwork Cases is over.

That night a burglar breaks into the Courtroom, searching for the coins that the lawyers had put into the Judge's slot. But he is soon disappointed; the Prosecutor and Defence Counsel—knowing, (like everyone else), that this would happen—had secretly slipped fake cardboard coins into the machine, before jabbing at the button marked 'A' . . . .

21
The Alchemist

An ageing Alchemist, alone among books and bubbling retorts, has—like all others of his profession, both now and at all times past—spent his life in the futile search for the Philosopher's Stone; which alone holds the magical means for transmuting lead into gold. Now, at last, he has abandoned his search. Instead, he turns his attention to another problem; that of turning gold—*into lead!* The idea excites him; he will leave his laboratory, travel throughout the world looking for gold on which to experiment. The whole Earth and its people will become his laboratory.

Naturally, in this he will fail; even more surely than he failed in his search before.

And even after his failure and death—which of course follow soon after—fate punishes him for his perversity. The gold statue of the Alchemist, erected by his colleagues on a high hill-top, is attacked by violent storms. Among winds and whirlwinds and flashes of lightning, flakes of gold-leaf fall from its face like autumn leaves—betraying, inch by inch, the grey dullness of lead beneath them . . . .

22
The Cheese Orgy

Bored by love, the Potentate commands an orgy of cheeses.

On the night appointed, a hand-picked dozen of girls are led from the harem into his palace. He awaits them in a high hall carpeted with parmesan. Candles mounted on stilton slices throw shadows flickering among the statues sculpted out of roquefort, and cherubs carved in camembert. Red rolls of cheese dangle from the ceilings. The girls spread themselves on soft yellow beds, moulded out of cheddar cheese. Slices of imported camembert mask their naked thighs. Long hair falls over their cheeks, cascading onto white shoulders and breasts shining in the candlelight. The sweet aromas of women and cheese intermingle with clouds of incense.

At the potentate's command music begins, played by an orchestra of blinded eunuchs. Scimitared slaves block all the entrances of the palace. Now the orgy commences. The Potentate sways sweating from girl to girl, biting and tongueing his way through the camembert. Their teeth nibble at his ears, while warm limbs intertwine writhing on beds of cheddar. Bodies sink rhythmically deeper into the cheese. He grunts over them, licking the gruyère off their conical nipples. Behind him a burly negress, powdered parmesan melting among her pubic hairs, bites into his buttocks. The girls surround him, their tongues furrowing the white cheese plastering his bald head and back. After hours of ecstasy they carry him, fat and exhausted, to a deep glass pool bubbling with milk. Here, after a rest, the orgy continues through that night and the night after. Naked figures splash and squeal in the cold milk, as it slowly turns yellow into butter, then into cheese. By the morning of the third night the butter has solidified. The potentate and his girls stand frozen inside a huge block of cheese. Only an occasional knee, a thigh, or a nipple stick out silently here and there from the sides of the block.

By order of the Potentate's son—who meanwhile—during the orgy, has seized power in a rapid coup d'état—the big block of cheese is hoisted out of the glass pool, carried from the palace, and displayed permanently in a new National Cheese Museum, built specially at his command . . . .

23
The Man Who Missed the Messiah

Excuse me sir, said a thin grey man plucking my sleeve in Jerusalem, could you please tell me when the Messiah is coming.

Why man, I said, haven't you heard? Don't you read the papers? He came yesterday, driving through this very street, at five o'clock in a white Cadillac, just as the Talmud said he would. What a sight it was! The crowds fighting through the police lines, trying to touch his halo and get a piece of his cloak. Women fainting three deep on the ground, men knocking one another down to get a better view. Well, he drove around for a while, giving out the odd blessing and so on, and granting Eternal Life to all of us who were there. Then he was off, up and away into the air in top gear. It's all in the papers, with pictures, this morning.

My god, moaned the little man, scratching the frown on his forehead, My god, I knew this would happen. Only yesterday I said to my wife—Wife, I said to her, how can I help you with the washing when any moment, perhaps today, the Messiah may come to Jerusalem. I've got to be ready to meet him, I said. But did she listen to a word I said?—not at all. Messiah Shmessiah, she said, now stop all this nonsense and get on with the washing. I tried to tell her about the Prophecy written in the Talmud, but she just said Rubbish! and hit me on the head with a wet scrubbing brush. So I did the washing, as she told me to. And now look what's happened, he sobbed, for a tub of dirty underwear I've missed the Millenium!

Hot steaming tears dropped all over me. He wiped his face on the front of my shirt, and buried his shaking head under my arm.

Not to worry, little man, I said, not to worry; there's more to the story. Just as he was leaving, the holy Mes-

siah rolled down the car window, leaned out and said—
Friends, brothers and sisters, he said, well—see you all
again. I'll be popping back from time to time to see how
you're getting on. And for those who missed this session,
and didn't manage to get any Eternal Life, tell them
they can get it all at my next visit. Don't know when
that'll be. Perhaps next year, perhaps the year after.
Read the Bible and the Talmud carefully, Friends, you'll
find my time-table in chapter six verse three.

When I had said this, the little man pulled his head
from under my arm and a wide smile spread across his
face. Thank you sir, he said.

Then radiant, his frown ironed out, he crossed the
streets of Jerusalem, climbed aboard a bus, and went back
home to his wife.

24
The Demonstration

Wearing long hair and arm-bands, we meet as arranged in the main square of the city. There are hundreds, perhaps thousands of us, some carrying posters, others without. Our leader today is the blond girl we call 'October-the-Fourteenth', named after the last day of the first revolution. As usual she wears to distinguish her a red mink stole, with an evening gown of red chiffon. At her signal, forming ranks ten-apiece, we march shouting and chanting down the long Main Street. Over our heads the banners flap like white eagles, guarding us from the sky. No one lines the streets, the shops are shuttered. The crowd snakes among deserted automobiles, their engines still ticking, towards the Presidential Palace at the far end. Suddenly around a corner we find our way blocked; steel barriers, like farm-gates, stretch across the street. Behind the barriers a wall of men with wide hips, thick arms—wearing black belts, gold buckles and buttons, blue uniforms, and riding boots; some of us see shuddering that the toes of these boots are well worn away . . . They have hard-domed helmets, and plastic visors through which we see pale faces refracted, distorted as through running water. They have guns, we do not—but then we have beards, and they have none. The crowd stops, piling up behind the leaders. Both sides know that the showdown has finally arrived. Led by October-the-Fourteenth we chant quicker, chant louder, link arms and move towards them; feet clatter across the cobbles, our fear forgotten. The barriers dissolve like water before us, men in blue uniforms scatter across the street. There is no shooting; their guns, of course, are made of plastic, bought cheaply in a toy shop off Main Street. Some—it is true—carry water pistols, but invariably they've forgotten to fill them. One waves a photo of himself on a beach, with a fat woman who he says is his wife—but everyone ignores his pleading. Others kneel in clumsy groups by the side of the street, building small shrines out of boots and handkerchiefs, under which they light candles and mumble prayers; but the shrines collapse, the hankies catch fire. Without smiling we wave away their bribes, pathetic offerings of peppermints and crumpled handkerchiefs. The way to the Presidential Palace is almost open; crowded behind our leader, sweat on our foreheads, we wait for the final act. Heavy silence fills the street. October-the-Fourteenth, brave as the day after which she is named, steps forward alone from the crowd, stands hands on her hips. Everyone, in both of the groups, is waiting for it to happen . . . Suddenly at last there is movement among the uniforms; the gold-braided Chief-of-Police stumbles across the gap towards us, towards our leader, pulling down his trousers as he runs. We see, without surprise, that his underpants are braided as well. October-the-Fourteenth throws us her stole, slips out of her evening gown of red chiffon. She wears no underwear; only the slogans of our party tattooed on her belly, her back, and each of her little breasts. They meet in the middle, intertwine, and fall to the ground. As they jerk and sigh on the cobbles, one on top of the other, we and the men in uniforms gather in a circle around them, clap rhythmically as the cry LONG LIVE THE REVOLUTION!! bursts from our throats, echoing among the streets up to the closed windows of the Presidential Palace . . . .

25
The Hara-Kiri Kit

A Japanese businessman, horn-rimmed and ambitious, decides to market a Hara-Kiri Kit.

Packaged in cellophane and painted cardboard, the price of the kit in Yen is neither too high nor too low for the average customer. It consists of the usual sword in stainless steel with a plastic handle, a patent leather sheath, and a full ceremonial robe (belted at the waist, disposable) in one of three sizes—Large, Medium, and Very Small. An enclosed Manual, printed on vellum, lists in alphabetical order all the Whens and Hows of Hara-Kiri—full instructions telling when, on what occasions, and how it is to be done. Also included, for beginners, is a plastic strip eighteen inches long, 'A' marked at one end, 'B' at the other, a dotted line in-between, which is taped to the abdomen as directed before inserting the sword at the point marked 'A'. Finally for a few Yen extra, your name is printed in pictographs on the box, the sheath, and the front of the robe itself.

Once production of the kits has begun, the advertising men take over:— NOW AT A PRICE EVEN *YOU* CAN AFFORD! blurb and blurbs, the posters, and the TV commercials. YOU DON'T HAVE TO BE AN ARISTO-CRAT!—scream huge orange letters across bill-boards. Now for the first time everyone, even the poor, can if necessary afford a suicide in the most traditional way of all. Soon Yen-waving crowds cram the shops and super-markets of the Hara-Kiri-Kit Company, all the way from Nagasaki up to Hirosaki. Shares climb as sales of the kit soar high above the clouds. Villas of the firm's directors multiply like mushrooms in the suburbs of Tokyo. But despite this everyone, especially the Director himself, somehow know that this cannot continue for long . . .

Suddenly one morning there is panic and shock at the Company's offices; a rival firm has hit the market! Every-where technicolour ads splatter the pages of the news-papers, fill the screens of the TV networks. A new company, the Hara-Kiri-Plasti-Co, offers at half the price, half the weight, a gift-wrapped kit for Hara-Kiri. The kit contains a sword of silver plastic, its sharpness tested re-tested and guaranteed; and the usual Sheath, Robes, Plastic Strip and Instruction Manual; but in addition they include an LP record of commentary and instructions for beginners, with traditional music in the background. Consternation fills the offices of the Hara-Kiri-Kit Co; shares have dropped and prices plunged. They are ruined, now bankruptcy knocks on the door. Sitting on the floor of the central office, the Director assembles his staff around him. They squat in silent rows while he reads out the accountant's last report. When he has finished, the Director sends one of his men down to the ware-house where the kits are stored. Bring back four dozen, he says, wiping his horn-rimmed glasses. But soon the man is back empty-handed and mumbling; something about 'all gone' . . . and 'taken by creditors' . . . reaches the Director's ears. Slowly he gets up and walks towards the telephone, which has not yet been disconnected. He looks for a phone number in a newspaper advert, dials, and then says—'Hara-Kiri-Plasti-Co? . . .' Meanwhile the others arrange themselves in waiting groups around the room. Someone busies himself in a corner, plugging a large record-player into the wall . . .

26
The Cloak

Who—of all our astronomers—could unravel the riddle of the universe? For who of them could imagine that all their observatories are only grains of sand, scattered here and there on the surface of an even greater grain of sand. Or that the Earth itself, with its wrinkled skin of seas and continents, floats and revolves in the clear matrix of a huge, cubic, black-sided box. Together with all other stars, suns and planets of our solar system, and of all the galaxies of the universe, it hangs suspended inside the box like bubbles in a block of perspex. This box, along with many others, is the property of a formless being whom—for want of a better word—we may call a 'Giant'. The Giant keeps these cubes piled carefully one on top of the other, in the cupboard of his room in a castle, which is one of many similar castles dotting the surface of the planet on which he lives. In each one lives another of the race of Giants who, like himself, owns a collection of these cubed black boxes in which galaxies of tiny planets contract, expand, or collide with one another. The darkness of each box is lit, from time to time, with a momentary glow as suns explode or comets collide. These box collections are not all of the same quality; there has always been much competition among the Giants as to whose collection is the biggest and whose is the best, and the boxes are often exchanged for one another. Most desirable of all are those boxes lit almost constantly with the flickering sparks of exploding universes, with the birth and death of solar systems. This world of lonely castles revolves through a galaxy of identical planets, dotted with the identical castles of other Giants. But this galaxy is not without an end—there is a point in space where its furthermost planet lies almost at the wall of the great black box, in which the galaxy itself is contained. This box is the favourite possession of an even more enormous Giant, who keeps it displayed—among other trinkets—in the ante-room of his capacious castle. From the window of his castle he can see no other castles, no other planets, like his own. He believes that he and his box are alone in the universe, which makes him feel quite proud. But of course he is wrong. What he thinks is his planet is, in reality, merely a microbe on the leg of a flea, climbing up the leg of an elephant, one of the millions of microbes on millions of fleas, climbing up the legs of a huge herd of elephants who trample and snort on a wide plain which ends—not in a horizon—but in the hard translucent wall of a vast demi-sphere, the flat surface of which is the plain itself. There are countless millions, perhaps more, of these demi-spheres. They lie in two parallel rows, one after the other, stretching infinitely away, the rows shifting slowly from side to side. They are the jewelled glittering buttons fixed to both edges of a long trailing Cloak whose entire length no-one,—not even the Wearer, the Great One Himself—has ever been able to measure . . . .

27
The Cigarette Man

He finds himself living in a King-Size cigarette, in a state of fear and apprehension.

He has tried to escape into the filter-tip, but his visa was not in order, and his passport long expired.

There are 19 other cigarettes in this packet of '20 KING-SIZE ROYAL FILTER-TIPPED CIGARETTES', and he wonders if any of the others are inhabited.

But there is no reply to his radio signals.

He knows that the fingers of the man in whose pocket he lies are stained with a yellowish blood. Also he knows that the Anti-Smoking Campaign of the government has been a failure.

He knows all the statistics.

Ever since birth his skin has feared statistics, and the fire, and the auto-da-fé.

The tobacco shreds around him are not sympathetic. We are all born to burn, they say fatalistically, and occupy themselves in a quiet, murmuring prayer.

Eventually his is the last cigarette remaining in the package. There is the rustle of the cellophane membrane, crackling like a flame. The tobacco shreds fall silent. He imagines the nemesis of sparks and sulphur, and the stink of burning flesh.

There is only one thing he can do; he dreams he is a monk immolating himself into ashes, into the Nirvana of fire. It is in a city, somewhere in Asia. He is aware of vast crowds kneeling in awe around him. He notices especially the women, how the reflections of the flames dance on their eyeballs. His smile in these reflections is charred and ecstatic. He burns like a sweet incense passing peacefully into the silence of a Great Temple. There is a sigh and a deep inhalation from the crowd as he changes slowly into flame, into smoke, and into a pile of black ashes smelling of gasoline.

The ashes are carefully collected, and placed in a huge gold ashtray, inlaid with valuable jewels.

Later they are transformed into a long, white, cylindrical reliquary. The reliquary is shaped like a cigarette, and lies alone in a packet marked 'KING-SIZE ROYAL FILTER-TIPPED CIGARETTES', in the pocket of a man with yellowed fingers. Maybe, in fact probably, this man has just given up smoking before the last cigarette could be smoked, but that doesn't really matter any more—for, in Asia, strange and terrified monks continue to appear from nowhere, and immolate themselves in the main squares of the cities. No one knows who these men are, or where they have come from. Their perfumed smoke-rings drift across the continent and across the world, from city to city, square to square.

Already, and everywhere, the ashtrays of the East are filling with the black ashes of these holy dreamers . . . .

28
The Emperor's Aversion

The Emperor of a certain far country (of which you have probably never heard), lives alone in a palatial palace painted with gold-leaf, on a hill overlooking his capital city.

Now this Emperor, for all his power, has one aversion more powerful than himself—he cannot bear the sight of poverty, and hence of beggars. He knows that if, even by mistake, his eye were to fall on anyone either poor or deformed, he would immediately sweat, feel faint, and fall frothing to the floor. Two weeks, at least, would then be required before he could rise from his featherbed again. For this reason he rarely, if ever, leaves his palace for the city in the plain below. Once a year however, on the anniversary of his coronation it is expected that he show his pale face to the people; otherwise, says his Chief Vizier, rumours might say he was dead . . .

He dreads that day for months before. In his nightmares, kneeling crowds of cripples pluck and pull at the hem of his robe, their sweat-smells rising to his nostrils despite his perfumed bath of the night before. He wakes retching in the mornings, consoled by his Court Physician, and repeats again the orders he has given every year, before every visit to the capital city. Guided by the Chief Vizier, the Emperor's army puts the plan into operation on the morning of the visit itself. In the blue dawn all the beggars are seized, grabbed, and pulled from hovels and alley-ways throughout the city. They are taken to special centres where, under the direction of Court Officials, they are stripped of their rags and crutches, bathed, shaved, perfumed, and dressed again in the finest finery from the wardrobe of the Emperor himself. Later— enveloped in ermine cloaks and collars, in gilt tiaras and coronets, jangling with bangles, bracelets, gems, jewels, and other baubles—the beggars are sworn to silence, then released. For that day, and that day only, they are to wear these clothes so as not, by their odious poverty, to offend the eye of the Emperor. Naturally, for fear of theft, the Chief Vizier has them watched discreetly by hordes of secret police, drafted specially from the provinces for the occasion.

Later that morning crowds of citizens jostle, flag-waving, in the streets as the Emperor rides through, is seen, is acclaimed, and returns flushed to his palace up a path paved with tiles of rare lapis-lazuli.

And also that day—a foreign traveller, passing for the first time through the capital city, remarks in his journal (published later as a famous book of exploration) on the curious nature of the aristocracy of that city; on the jewelled magnificence of their clothes and coronets, but also on their strangely misshapen forms. He writes of blind Barons, hunchbacked Earls, Dukes toothless and tubercular, on the matted hair of grey Duchesses, and above all on their strange habit of plucking at the sleeves of passers-by, holding out their hands sparkling with ruby rings, almost as if—in some silent way—they were trying to ask something of him . . . .

29
The Proverb

At the foot of the blue mountains, the warm dry sands of Arabia wash over the last monument to the sage Ibn Yasir. It rests among winds and emptiness, a solitary pillar of blue-veined marble, now fractured by time, its cracks oozing with the reddish dust of the desert. One of the thousands erected to the memory of Ibn Yasir—that ancient mysterious figure of whom so little is known; who has left behind no books, no testaments, and no disciples. We know only this, that in his entire life he produced only one work of importance—a single Proverb written down, it is said, a few hours before his death. Yet this Proverb was the purest essence of all the sage's wisdom; within its delicate frame of words it contained ideas powerful enough to burst men's minds into flame. After his death the power of these words flew like a desert storm through the cities and tents of Arabia. Those who read the Proverb, and studied its meaning, were transformed; they became new and wiser men, living their lives by its message. Around its wisdom they fashioned new religions and vast empires, spreading its radiance across the mountains into other lands. Monuments to Ibn Yasir and to his Proverb sprouted on the hill tops. In every city, libraries swelled with books of interpretation and commentary; academics devoted only to commenting on these commentaries, multiplied like fungi. Yet strangely enough, though these countless books have been written about it, and though it has sculptured the lives of generations, the actual words of the Proverb, and even its meaning, have long been forgotten. Some say it was very short, perhaps only a few words long, but even of this we cannot be sure; no record, no trace of the Proverb remains. True, several versions of it do survive in various commentaries, but no two versions ever agree; nor can these books, written centuries after Ibn Yasir's death, be considered reliable. So the original Proverb is lost somewhere in the depths of time. The books of commentary which had reflected its brilliance, and the cities in which they were housed, have dried and crumbled away. With the cycle of centuries, the empires built upon it have sunk into the sands. The winds of Arabia have wiped it off monuments, and blown away the bones of all who had ever read it. Only its echo remains, a vague murmur among the empty ruins.

It was once carved high on this lonely pillar, so that all desert travellers who read it could pass refreshed on their silent way among the dunes. But even here, though it is the last monument of all, hardly a trace of the Proverb remains. On the grey furrowed marble only the words 'Behold' . . . 'Peacock' . . . and 'Shadow' . . . can be vaguely deciphered. But below where the Proverb had been inscribed you can still read the following inscription —the last words spoken by Ibn Yasir—cut into the marble in a faint, cursive Arabic—

> 'If you have read this Proverb,
> And grasped its meaning,
> Then that is the proof
> That you have not really understood it—
> Since only those
> Who can truly understand the Proverb
> Never will have need to read it,
> Nor even to understand its meaning—'

30
The Marshmallow Rocketship

A rocket scientist, who used to work in a confectionery, designs a spacerocket constructed entirely of marshmallows and milk chocolate. His idea briefly, is that this arrangement will save space which, otherwise, would be taken up by food. As all four astronauts have a 'sweet tooth' they can chew away at the walls of the spacecraft on the journey to Venus, and on the way back. And as they fatten on their marshmallow diet, the inner walls of the craft will be eaten thinner and thinner. Then everything will fit snugly together. Truly, the confectionery-man-turned-scientist has thought of everything! Well, after the design has been scrutinized by certain fat men in horn-rimmed glasses, and approved by other fat men in horn-rimmed glasses, the rocket is built, launched, and zooms dramatically into space. At blast-off, above the roar of the rear engines, can be heard the intense and synchronised munching of the four astronauts inside.

So, months pass, and even years, without sign or signal from the milk chocolate and marshmallow spacecraft. After a while, the fat horn-rimmed men commission the confectioner-scientist to build another spacecraft to search for the first one. Four new sweet-toothed astronauts are carefully selected and trained for the expedition. This time the spacecraft is cunningly constructed of chocolate fudge with marzipan fins. And once again, among the roar of rockets, and the rhythmic crunching of teeth, the craft is shot off into space. And once again it fails to return—and has not returned until this very day, even though hundreds of other rockets, crammed with munching astronauts have been launched to look for it and for each other. The scientist tries peppermint rockets, chocolate eclair rockets, rockets built of strawberry cake and toasted meringue, and many, many others. But . . . all to no avail. What has happened to the rockets? Are they lost in a new dimension? Have they collided with shooting stars? Have the astronauts developed tooth-ache? The scientist gibbers and sweats in his nightly nightmares.

Well, the truth is more prosaic, and can be easily dis-covered if you should wander into a Venusian super-market, and stop at the giant counter with a sign saying (in Venusian)—'CONFECTIONERY, EXOTIC CANDIES SOLD HERE'. Look for the large candies with the curious munching sound inside. They're expensive but, believe me, they taste Good!

31
TheThree Disguised Invasions of Earth

On their First Invasion of Earth, the Martians arrive disguised as Dentists (a disguise chosen through one of their telescopes). Once having landed, they stroll in vast white-coated crowds through the streets, many thousands of them, all wearing identical bifocal glasses, whistling unobtrusively, and casually accosting passers-by and drilling their teeth on the spot. To their surprise, people see through this disguise, and soon the Martians are all efficiently wiped out by the Secret Police—who also liquidate all the real dentists they can find, mistaking them for Martians . . .

(From this last mistake, several years of toothache result.)

On their Second Invasion of Earth, knowing sadly now the fallibility of human disguises, the Martian shock-troops land in a new guise—From their spacecraft pour a multitude of roosters, hens, ganders and geese, not to mention ducks and drakes, all cunningly disguised in authentic beaks and feathers; and every cluck and cock-a-doodle-do has been carefully rehearsed. This time their disguise is perfect. Only one detail is out of place; namely, that they land in an area of Earth inhabited neither by man nor fowl, but by certain other creatures whom the little feathered Martians greet in a cheerful and familiar fashion . . .

(What happened to the Second Martian Invasion, you may ask. Don't ask me—ask the wolves.)

Well, by their Third Invasion, the Martians have learnt a thing or two. No longer will they rely on feathered or bifocal disguises. Instead, they build their spacecraft as exact replicas of one of the everyday objects scattered about the surface of Earth; an ordinary common object, so ordinary that nobody will even notice them lying around. But meanwhile, inside that object—millions of shock-troops, armed, ruthless, and undisguised, waiting for the signal to attack. Everything is ready—the Martians prepare the craft, cram them with enthusiastic troops, and rocket them down to Earth.

Next morning, hundreds of huge tin cans—each one an enormous cylinder, fifty stories high—lie scattered about the Earth in parks and in deserts, squeezed between skyscrapers, and blocking the sunrise over the suburbs. And across each one, in red and golden letters a hundred feet high, the words—'SPITZ'S BAKED BEANS IN TOMATO SAUCE' glitter in the dawn.

And once again, to the Martians' amazement, everyone notices them—even though they're disguised as everyday objects. Soon they are surrounded by screams, shouts, tanks and planes. While the panicky Martians inside, realising their plan has failed, prepare for blast-off again—a strange thing happens—all the planes and tanks are suddenly withdrawn, and in the new silence can be heard the voices of envious advertising executives saying to one another—'Not bad, not bad at all!', 'Gee, wish I'da thought of that gimmick myself!' and 'Wonder which agency handled that Spitz's contract, lucky bastards!'

'Advertising agency?!' says Spiro P. Spitz III, Company President, to the interviewers—'don't you believe it; it was *me* that thought of the gimmick. Sure boys, it was all my idea, those big tin cans. Ask my wife Fanny here. It was all my idea, wasn't it Fanny? See! Best advertising gimmick you boys ever seen, I betcha!'

And while the shares of Spitz's Canned Goods Inc. snake upwards on the stock-markets, the first purple tentacles snake out of the little portholes under the words—'SPITZ'S BAKED BEANS IN TOMATO SAUCE' . . . .

32
The Psychiatric Anteater

Looking at me now, you would think that I was an ordinary Anteater. But of course you'd be wrong. Actually, I'm a psychiatrist—perhaps the only Anteater Psychiatrist in the world. Certainly I'm the only one in this zoo, and in the city which lies around it. For that reason I am regarded by the other Anteaters here as being rather peculiar. To them my answer has always been— each one to his own vocation; tolerate me and I'll tolerate you. Let them think I'm much too sentimental, let them spend their time entertaining tourists with tongue acrobatics—if they're so insensitive to the suffering, the real mental suffering, of our world, then that is their problem—not mine. Being, I might say, more aware than the others, my task is to alleviate this suffering. That is why I became a psychiatrist.

I hold my clinic here at the zoo, in the cage in which I am sitting. Every morning a bigger crowd gathers at the bars to look and point as I take my daily psycho-therapeutic session. Word has obviously got around to them already what a competent psychiatrist I am. The sessions begin about eight o'clock when the keeper brings in the first of my patients. They are let into the cage through a tiny gate in the wire. Generally there are several thousand of them. At first they are naturally confused; some are hysterical, while others are quiet or catatonic. I let them get a bit used to me before I settle down to the serious business of diagnosis and treatment. First I must separate off the psychotics from the simple anxiety neuroses. This isn't very difficult to do. The psychotics are easily diagnosed by their complete refusal to face up to reality and to adjust to their situation. For example, very soon after they are put into my cage— into my clinic—they try to escape! Also, they refuse to acknowledge that I'm only there to help them, and often they become quite frantic in trying to get away from me. All my research has shown that there is nothing

I can do for these patients; they are without any hope of cure, neither psychotherapy nor all the drugs in my repertoire can do anything to help them. Having lost Reality they live entirely in their own darknesses. And therefore their therapy, which takes place once I have rounded them all up, must be more drastic. Usually this part of my session is very popular with the crowd; people clap and cheer and press their faces to the bars. Sometimes at this stage I can even be persuaded to take a little bow, but in general I try to maintain an air of professional distance.

When I have finished this, I turn my attention back to the neurotics. Now the really skillful part of the therapy begins; for I must get their confidence, break the hold of their fears and inhibitions, and gradually lead them back to an acceptance of Reality. They must learn to adjust to the realities of their situation. There are certain technical problems in doing this—not the language problem, you understand,—but the fact that my patients are so small, with such fragile voices (which in any case are often distorted by fear) that it is some-times difficult to get a proper case-history out of them. Still, I am patient and try to do my best. Firstly, I lay my long nose down among them and they swarm curiously between the bristles on my face. Then we be-gin talking frankly to one another. I tell them my problems, they tell me theirs. Eventually I enquire, in some detail, as to their early relationships with their parents, any traumatic happenings in their childhoods, and so on. Sometimes we discuss their hidden hopes and phobias, what they are secretly afraid of, and try to analyse what prevents them adjusting to reality. With time they begin to feel easier with me, and to realize that my only concern is to diminish their suffering; in short, they learn to regard me as a friend. When they are feeling more relaxed, and the group therapy is well under way, and when despite all the inhibitions in their psyches, my little patients and I are nearer to a mutual understanding, and to an acceptance of the situation in which they find themselves—then they are ready for the final act of my therapy. Gently I ask them to line up in long rows. This they quickly do; line upon line of by now well-adjusted patients, all cheerful and relaxed. their phobias long forgotten. Then I slide the long pinkness of my tongue across the cage's floor, and with some even singing they step smartly onto it. Soon they have formed themselves into ordered ranks, blackening the surface on my tongue. Now the crowd applauds wildly— I draw my tongue up slowly into my mouth—my lips meet—and then there is silence; the clinic is ended and the big crowd wanders away. My psychotherapy for the day is over.

33
The Ark

Abandoned by God, the ark floats aimlessly and empty on a plain of sea. Only Noah and the lions remain. There are many lions, multiplying as fast as the forty years since the Flood began. All the other animals aboard, all the flesh and fowl, have either eaten, or been eaten by one another. Even the men have died; drowned, one by one, beneath the years.

Noah, alone now among the roars, stands on the splintered wood of the upper deck. The lions circle below, thoughtfully, searching for the stairs of the gangway up. Over him creak the' riggings, to which tired generations of doves have returned, every evening—their beaks empty.

The sky reddens. At the foot of the gangway the lions crowd for the final rush, jostling among themselves. Suddenly, small shadows fall over their faces; from every horizon white clouds of doves flow towards the ark. Even through old eyes, Noah can see how each dove holds in its beak an olive branch, a crumb, or a piece of cloth. They swoop down joyfully towards him—

The lions and doves hold Noah, for a long instant, like a plucked flower between two soft fingers . . . .

34

The Poetry Fish

for Leslie

My brother, who is a fisherman, is the dreamer of our village. Ever since I can remember he has had visions; he has watched the mountains breathe, seen the birds carrying thunder-clouds on their backs, and listened in always to the green conversations of the trees. But for all this he is a gentle man, without guile, and so I was careful not to hurt his feelings that evening when he told me of the poetry fish that he'd caught the day before. We had heard often of the finding of these fish, of course, especially in the tales told to us when we were children, but I have never really believed that they existed—nor that one could ever be caught by a fisherman. So although the others laughed at him, as they usually do, I was the one who agreed to go with him to the harbour to see the fish. On the way there he told me more. Not only had he caught the fish the day before, but at the end of every day for the past few weeks he had found one of these fishes struggling in his nets. Each time he had thrown it back into the ocean, but this time he had kept one for me to see. When I had seen it, he said, when I was sure that his dreams were as real as life, then he would return it to the sea.

In the harbour, sheltered by a curtain of hills, we came on his solitary boat with the blue eye painted on its prow. It was moored far from the forest of masts, its sails swaying slowly in the breeze. The harbour was empty of people; only the silence of dusk, the slow creaking of the mooring ropes, and the gentle blue splashing of the sea. He climbed down the narrow steps before me. I could see the sky reflected on the bottle he had brought out from under the boat's tarpaulin. He held it out for me to see smiling, I think, at the expression on my face. I looked inside it, fingered the glass, and held it up to the rays of the sun. Even through the muddy water the fish glowed gold in the twilight. It had fins of amber, streaked with coral red, and its delicate tail, transparent as crystal, waved slowly through the water around and around. There was nothing more for me to say; I avoided my brother's eyes. Then for the first time, I read the poem marked in black characters on the gold scales of its back. One line after another I read as the fish circled the bottle. The words of the poem seemed to come echoing out of the deep green caverns, rising to my eyes from among shifting fields of anemones. We read it again and again, till the day died and the fish's light faded away; and then we slipped it back into the dark waters.

That was the first of the poetry fish that my brother showed to me. Each of their poems was a mosaic of images, a strange and delicate web of beauty, which has left its echo inside me even to this day. But from then on my brother began to change. He has always been, in many ways, a simple man, but the rhythms of poetry that he had learnt from these fish had transformed him. His manner, once blurred and distant, became more confident and clear. He would sit before our house in the dusk telling of the poems he had found in the sea that day. At first the villagers laughed at him, as they have always done, but then gradually they began to understand the meanings of his words. Every evening the crowd of listeners grew bigger around him. Soon he was becoming known as a master poet not only in our village, but in all the villages nearby, and indeed word had even reached the Capital City of the fisherman-poet who told his poetry every evening in an obscure village square. Few of the people still laughed in his presence now; only when he tried to tell them that he hadn't written the poems, that he'd found them on the backs of the poetry fish that he'd caught, would they nudge one another, and giggle and snigger behind their hands. The more he tried to explain, the louder the villagers laughed, roaring till their eyes watered as they stumbled back to their houses.

One evening near the harbour I met him carrying a covered bottle towards the village. Through its cover I could see the moving glow of a poetry fish. I knew clearly then what would happen, and warned him against doing it, but he was angry and determined and pushed past me without a word. In the square before our house, the crowd waiting to hear him was bigger than ever. As on the other evenings, he sat down among them and told of the poem he had found that day. They listened in silence, but when he had finished he brought out the bottle and put it on the ground before him. Then he explained, as he had many times before, that the poems that they'd heard from him were poems from the backs of golden fish that he had found in his nets each day, and that in this bottle he had one of these fish for them to see. There was nothing I could do to stop him; he uncovered the bottle and pushed it towards them. We looked inside it. The fish was dead, its limp floating body as brown as the earth. And on its back only a mottled blur where once the words had been. No one in the crowd said anything. As they moved silently away, someone picked it out of the bottle and threw it in a high arc through the air to where the dogs were waiting.

Since that day he has never caught another poetry fish. Yet every day still he searches in his little boat through the plains of the sea. But in the evenings, even if his nets are filled, there is no sign of amber fins among the catch. He has become thin, old despite his youth, with the search for the poetry fish. He is rarely at home, rarely in the village. Even the poems have left him, as they have left me—only a word, perhaps a phrase, remains echoing in our minds.

One day, when he has found the poetry fish again, he will return no longer to his home, not even to the land itself. He says he has begun to hear the thunder echoing in the deep green caverns, calling him down to the shifting fields of anemones.

35
The Square Banana

'I sure see Love as a Square Banana' said the man next to me in the wharfside bar, curling an embittered lip around his double-gin, 'Love is also like an artichoke on wheels, which you're just beginning to eat when the brakes fail! Some men regard it as an empty carrot, or a many-layered onion, but as for me—O yeh, Man—I see Love as a goddam SQUARE BANANA!' So spoke this thoughtful man, pouring himself another drink and puking here and there over the counter, before continuing his vegetarian soliloquy, though the bar was exceptionally crowded that night with noise and men and women, too. Then suddenly, as I recall, there emerged from among the barsmoke and bottle-clinks a woman's voice, pointed right in my direction, shouting—'Hey, Mister, has he been giving you all that vegetable shit?—all that crap about Artichokes and Love and all that?—Don't listen to him, Mister, after three gins he's like that. Every Time!'

The man with the lip twists around, dropping his gin onto my bare toes, and yells in bloodshot tones—'Shut your goddam face, woman—can't I even talk to my friend here without you butting in?!'—'You shut up, too!' says the woman's voice back fiercely, '*You* shut your big mouth, Frank, not me'—and O then, before I or anyone could stop him, Frank hits and punches a slurred way through barsmoke maze and double-faces, with me behind, parting the people round the bar-counter like fragile corn—till at last we can see, with his eyes and mine, the owner of that same woman's voice—Frank's woman. And there she is—and, folks, you know what—she's square and yellow in colour all over! or rather cubic shaped, but extremely yellow on every surface, she is—yellow like a jaundiced sunflower. And there's black marks all over her, and a big green stalk bulging out one corner of the cube. And the man jumps himself on her, and now she is whimpering in her yellow square voice—

61

'O Frank, O no Frank—Not here, Frank'—and him rough and grabbing at the corner of her yellow square, near the stalk, as he peels off the thick surface most fluently,—rips off, in the sudden silence, the square skin from one of her sides, and there inside of her is Softness,—lighter-yellow in colour—and then she is screaming—'O please Frank, No!'—as he scoops big handfuls of the soft mush into his mouth, into his stomach, gurgling fancifully as he empties her out, mouthful by mouthful. And all the while the rest of us are looking here and there, embarrassedly, and asking the time of one another, as her voice gets thinner and thinner and fades away while he scoops her out, and swallows her down, and pukes now and again, and sips a little gin between mouthfuls with a strange smile over his face. Then he's finished, and no-one meets his eye as he picks up the limp yellow skin off the floor, and throws it over his shoulder like an empty sack. And from the skin her weak voice—'Aw shucks, honey—Why do we *have* to go through this every time?—it's wearing me down—' and him gently saying—'C'mon—C'mon now baby—Don't talk now, baby—We're going home now baby—It's all over now—' and carrying her wrinkled yellowness through the crowd and into the outside night.

Nobody says nothing as they leave the bar, though bottles clink a little louder for a while, and a yellowish taste lingers in our mouths . . . .

36
The Rooftop

Broke up with my woman, of a sudden, one morning, my best friend too—ripped the postcard they sent me into a million technicolour pieces and smashed her black-and-white smile on the mantlepiece—but still didn't feel any better. Flushed down her lawyer's letter, and the Mortgage and the gas bill, and the food bills and TV repair bills and all the other bills I couldn't pay and stared for a week at the blurred ceiling. Felt lower and sadder those days than a dog's turd squashed on a sidewalk.

No money and no woman, an no nothing left for me.

So I decided to kill myself.

But no barbiturates were left in the bottle, and the gas had been cut off, and all razor blades blunt in the house, so I took one final taxi to the tallest skyscraper in town, intending to throw myself off its most upper and in-accessible floor, and splatter myself thereby on a side-walk cold as my gone woman's heart.

Took a crowded elevator up to the top floor of the building, my face wet and salty, and climbed out onto the rooftop, pushing my way among the mob of people standing there, to fling myself utterly off the ledge and into infinity and the morning newspapers.

But only two feet had I pushed before thick hands encircled my arm, and a square-chinned voice murmured slow in my ear—'Hey, friend, where do you think you're going. Can't you see there's a queue up here—?' Well, guess that's what I hadn't noticed before; namely that the Rooftop was bulging with a huge and murmuring crowd, all patiently queueing for their chance to throw them-selves off that one-time Ledge.—

So I took my place in that selfsame Queue—and that's where I'm still today.

There are thousands of us up here, sardine-packed among the water-tanks and the TV aerials; every age and inclination, and colour, too. We've got a pretty good crowd on our Rooftop, and we manage a lot of fun together. Got ourselves organized into committees, into Bridge clubs and Bingo groups, and into Keep-Fit and Yoga classes. There's free hairdo's for the ladies twice a day, and regular lessons in First Aid. We've got two football teams chosen now (but no space to play in) and there's a weekly swimming competition in one of the water tanks. Even scratched together a jazz band and two pop groups, and they help out on the music side of the five bars and overcrowded discotheque we've got located on the Rooftop. We get daily soda-water and blackberry pie, and sometimes six- or seven-course meals brought up here by our next-of-kin,—and they bring us regular love movies, too.

Otherwise, not much happens up here. Sometimes we're pretty bored and there's nothing left to do but listen to those once-a-day thuddings on the sidewalks, and the wail of sirens, and the claps and shriekings of the crowd below; or else count the ambulance-lights as they converge around us every morning.

Of course, we're not alone up here in the sky; through binoculars we've seen how every other Rooftop in the city (and maybe in every other Rooftop in the world) is crammed with folks just like ourselves waiting for a chance to jump off. We keep up regular contact with some of these other Rooftops—send them our weekly newsletter, and they send us theirs. Also, we've noticed over time that these mobs in the streets below are gradually evaporating away, as more and more of the citizenry crowd up stairs and elevators to join us in the massed queues on the Rooftops.

As for Jumping-Off Times:—while some of the Rooftops are organized by ballot, we on our Rooftop have arranged things on a First-come, First-served basis. By this scheme, my chance off The Ledge should come in— let's see—about forty-three years time, I calculate.

In the meantime, I'm working away up here—in my spare time—on the Third and Fourth Volumes of my Suicide Note . . . .